NIC BISHOP
BIG CATS

Scholastic Press / New York

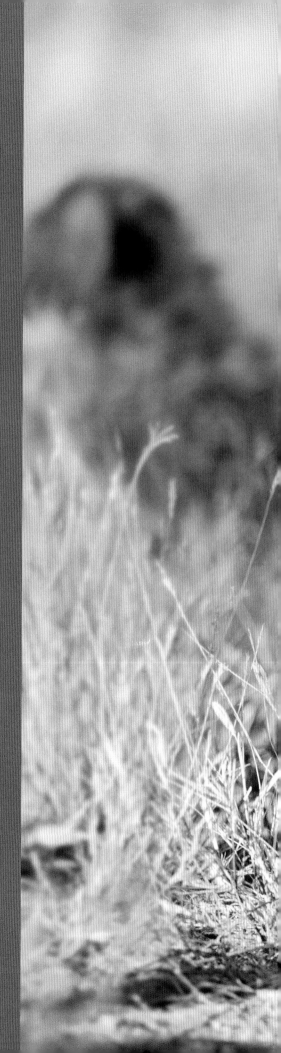

LIBRARY OF CONGRESS CATALOGING-IN-PUBLICATION DATA
Names: Bishop, Nic, 1955- author, photographer.
Title: Big cats / Nic Bishop.
Description: New York : Scholastic Press, 2019. | Audience:
   Ages 7-10. | Audience: Grades 4 to 6.
Identifiers: LCCN 2017061554 | ISBN 9780545605779 (hc)
   | ISBN 9780545605847 (ebk)
Subjects: LCSH: Panthera—Juvenile literature. | Felidae—Juvenile
   literature. | CYAC: Cats.
Classification: LCC QL737.C23 B5745 2019 | DDC 599.75/5—dc23
LC record available at https://lccn.loc.gov/2017061554

10 9 8 7 6 5 4 3 2 1   19 20 21 22 23

Printed in Malaysia   108
First printing, October 2019

The text type was set in 13.5-pt. Bawdy Bold.
The display type was set in ITC Franklin Gothic
Condensed Std Demi Extra Condensed.
The book was printed and bound at Tien Wah Press.
Production was overseen by Jael Fogle.
Manufacturing was surpervised by Shannon Rice.
Book was designed by Marijka Kostiw

For help with taking some of the photographs I wish
to thank the Cheetah Conservation Fund, Khao
Kheow Open Zoo, and the Clouded Leopard Consortium.
I would also like to thank Bill Wood, Project Manager
of the Clouded Leopard Consortium, for his kind help.

*Title page: Scientists believe the size and color of a lion's mane
help show how strong and healthy he is. A rival male should
avoid a male with a good mane.*

This page: Cheetah cub.

A cat can tread silently on the soft pads of its toes,

slipping from sunlight to shadow like a ghost. It will follow prey for hours, watching, waiting, and staying unseen. Then it pounces with unstoppable power. Grace and guile turn suddenly to raw muscle and razor claws.

Cats are carnivores. They hunt and eat other animals. There are about forty different types of cats, from five-hundred-pound tigers to ten-pound fluffy house cats that curl up on your lap. The smallest cat is the rusty-spotted cat of South Asia. It weighs less than four pounds.

The tiger lives in southern and southeastern Asia, as well as Siberia. It is the largest of all cats. An adult male can weigh about 500 pounds, although there have been reports of animals that have weighed more than 700 pounds.

This book is about the largest and most powerful of all cats.

They are called big cats and include tigers, lions, jaguars, leopards, snow leopards, and clouded leopards. We will also learn about pumas and cheetahs. They are more closely related to smaller cats, and can purr like your pet kitty. But they are as large as big cats. So in this book we will refer to them all as big cats.

Pumas live in North and South America. They are known by many names, including mountain lion, cougar, and catamount. Like most big cats, pumas spend much of their lives alone.

Most big cats prefer to hunt during the twilight hours of dusk and dawn, as well as at night.

They may walk for miles between sunset and sunrise, patrolling a home range in which they know every trail, resting place, and feeding ground of their prey. Often they prowl near waterholes and other places where prey gathers, waiting for an opportunity to strike.

Leopards live in Africa and parts of Asia. They are one of the stealthiest big cats. A leopard often studies its prey's movement from a distance and then silently creeps close to cut it off in an ambush.

Most big cats cannot chase prey very far. So they stalk until they are as close as possible, usually within ten to twenty yards. A leopard, for example, will often not attack until it is just five yards from its target. It cleverly uses every bump and hollow, every bush and blade of grass, to conceal its approach.

As the big cat creeps close it concentrates on every movement of its prey, calculating just when to advance or freeze. **Then it explodes in a fearsome rushing charge.** A lion or tiger can sprint at about thirty-five miles per hour and leap more than twenty feet onto its victim, slapping it to the ground with powerful forelegs.

The Amur, or Siberian, tiger, has thicker fur than other tigers to help it survive the freezing cold winters in eastern Russia and China. It hunts moose, musk deer, wild boar, and even bears.

Every second counts in the attack.

A single mistake can mean serious injury from the prey's thrashing hooves and horns. But big cats are quick to subdue their victims. Their long claws, which are normally retracted in their paws for protection, flick out like grappling hooks to snag flesh. Saber-like canine teeth pierce and hold the struggling animal, giving it little chance of escape.

This yawning lion is showing off its huge canine teeth. These can be about three inches long, to penetrate the skin of animals and hold on. Lions are found in Africa and parts of India. Even though they are powerful hunters, they can also be scavengers, feeding on prey that has been killed by other animals, such as hyenas and leopards.

As soon as it can, the cat will clamp its jaws on the prey's windpipe to suffocate it. Or it might bite the back of the neck, through the spine. **The jaguar has extremely powerful jaws, which can bite right through its victim's skull.**

Big cats are such skilled hunters that most can bring down prey three times their own weight, and sometimes even greater. More amazing is that they usually do this alone. Unlike wolves and hyenas, which hunt in groups, most big cats are solitary hunters. But hunting is never easy. It is very hard to sneak up on a deer or antelope without being seen. Often, the prey will get away and the cat must try again. A big cat needs patience, as well as skill.

Jaguars are the third-largest big cat, after tigers and lions. They are found in South America and southern parts of North America. Their prey includes tapirs, capybaras, deer, caimans, turtles, and sometimes even anacondas.

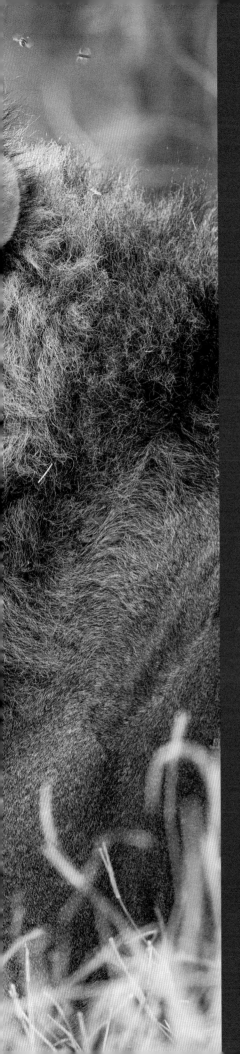

The tiger is the biggest and most powerful big cat. Its striped coat hides it perfectly, especially in tall grass, so it can sneak up on deer, wild boar, and buffalo. Tigers in India are known to kill huge, wild, ox-like animals called gaur, which can weigh 2,000 pounds. **Lions may take down bigger prey because they are the only big cats that hunt in family groups, called prides.** African prides are made of mothers, daughters, sisters, aunts, and their cubs, along with one or two adult males. They can work as a group to single out and overwhelm powerful animals like buffalo. The largest prides may have thirty lions, which is enough to take on a hippopotamus, or perhaps even an elephant.

This African male lion is eating an eland. A large kill like this can feed a big cat for a week, leaving time for catnapping before the next hunt. Lions sleep for sixteen to twenty hours a day.

The cheetah lives in Africa and the Middle East. Its long legs and flexible spine make it a fast sprinter, but it does not have the brute strength of other big cats. Therefore it prefers to hunt prey less heavy than itself.

Cheetahs catch animals in a different way than other big cats. They usually hunt during the day and chase after their victim. They will stalk until they are within about seventy yards of their prey and then sprint at breakneck speed.

The cheetah's supple spine lets it take running strides of up to twenty-three feet. Its heart, lungs, and breathing passages are extra large, to help power it to around sixty-five miles per hour.

That is the fastest running speed of any land animal.

Unlike other cats, the cheetah's claws stay out as it runs, gripping the soil for quick twists and turns. Its long tail helps, too, swinging like a rudder so the cheetah can outmaneuver its target. As it draws close, the cheetah reaches out its front paw to swat the prey's hind legs, tripping it headfirst into a tumble. Then the cheetah strikes.

Despite its speed, a cheetah catches prey only about half the time.

It can sprint for just a few hundred yards before it starts to tire.

If the chase is long, the exhausted cheetah will eventually collapse into

the grass, with its rib cage pumping to recover its breath.

Even when a cheetah succeeds, it may still lose its prize.

Larger lions and leopards will steal a cheetah's food if they can. But

cheetahs, like all cats, can eat a lot and eat fast. At the back of their

mouths, where you have teeth called molars, they have carnassials.

These teeth have sharp edges that slice like scissors to bite off chunks

of meat. Cats also have sharp bristles, called papillae, on their tongues

to lick meat from bones. These papillae also help a cat clean its fur when

it licks itself. A cheetah can swallow up to thirty pounds in one big

meal. A lion may gulp down as much as seventy pounds. After a large

feast a big cat will not need to hunt for several days.

The cheetah hunts mostly during the day, so unlike other big cats, it does not need good night vision. Nevertheless, its day vision is fearsomely sharp. A cheetah can spot a small gazelle moving more than a mile away.

Leopards are secretive and rarely seen in the open. This African leopard was taking a short break at sunset before heading into the night to hunt.

A leopard, too, can have its food stolen by a lion or some hyenas.

But it has a trick. **Leopards are expert climbers and strong enough to haul their prey up a tree using just their mouths.**

There they can eat in safety. Leopards are very widespread and are also adaptable to different environments. They live in Africa and parts of Asia as far north as Siberia. They hunt in forests, grasslands, dry scrublands, and even in some cities. Some have black fur, particularly those living in the dense forests of Southeast Asia. Scientists are not certain how dark fur is helpful to these leopards, which are often called black panthers. Perhaps it hides them among the deep shadows of the trees.

Jaguars sometimes have black fur, too, and in many ways they look like leopards. But jaguars have a heavier build and are found in South America. They also live in parts of Mexico and have even been spotted in southwestern parts of the United States, such as Arizona and New Mexico. Jaguars prefer to hunt in forests and are often near water. Like tigers, they enjoy swimming. Pumas also live in parts of the Americas. They are found from as far north as Canada to Patagonia in southern Chile, living in forests, deserts, and even high in the Andes Mountains.

Pumas hunt many different animals, from tiny mice to large deer such as elk.

Pumas have powerful hind legs that make them good jumpers. They have been reported to leap almost forty feet horizontally.

Almost everything about a big cat makes it a successful predator.
Those that hunt at night have eyes that can see about six times
better than yours. A big cat's ears can swivel to pinpoint the
tiniest rustle of movement. **Really, prey has little chance.**

All cats walk on their toes. Touch-sensitive hairs on their
feet allow them to quietly place each paw without looking down.
They also have sensitive whiskers, called vibrissae, near their
mouths and eyes. These detect nearby objects, helping a cat
move easily and silently through dense vegetation in the darkness.
The whiskers also feel the prey's shape when the cat attacks and
help target just where to bite.

Leopards have long whiskers to help them feel their way among branches in the treetops and on the forest floor. This leopard was about to leap into a tree to hide an impala. But hyenas stole its prey before it could haul the impala to safety.

Cats also have a good sense of smell, but they use it to "message" each other more than to find prey.

Cats communicate with scent glands on their bodies, particularly their heads and paws. When a cat rubs its head on something or scrapes it with its paw, it leaves a scent message to tell others it has visited.

The same happens when a cat sprays scented urine. If another cat smells this it can probably tell several things. For example, it might know how long ago the scent was left, whether it came from a female or a male, or from a cat it knows or a stranger. It might even learn about the age and health of the cat.

These lions greeting each other are probably brothers. Head rubbing may be a way of sharing scents and bonding between pride members.

Scent messages are also used to mark a cat's territory. They allow neighbors to check each other out without coming face-to-face. Meeting is usually a bad idea for cats.

They can viciously defend their territories against strangers.

Male big cats may even fight to the death.

Big cats communicate with calls, too. Lions, tigers, jaguars, and leopards roar to announce themselves and warn rivals away from their territories. Lions can probably hear each other roar from a distance of about five miles. Big cats make other calls such as coughs, grunts, snarls, and yelps, but the nicest is known as the prusten call. This is made by tigers, jaguars, snow leopards, and clouded leopards. It is a soft, affectionate call of recognition, sometimes also called chuffing. It is often made between a mother and her cubs.

The Amur leopard lives in eastern Russia and China. It grows long, thick fur to survive during freezing cold winters.

When a big-cat mother is ready to give birth she finds a safe place for a den. It might be a rocky cave, a hollow log, or a group of bushes. Snow leopards may use a secret shelter high on a mountain cliff. A lioness may find one among tall grasses. It is important that the cubs are hidden from predators because the mother will raise them alone. Male big cats do not help.

The cubs are also born blind and remain so for the first one to two weeks.

Their mother will leave them to hunt nearby, but she returns often to suckle them.

The mother always stays vigilant. At any sign of danger she will pick up each cub with her mouth and carry it by the back of the neck to a new den. She may change dens several times to keep her young safe.

This clouded leopard cub is about two months old and actively exploring its surroundings. On average most big cats have two to four cubs, though cheetahs usually have three to five.

These cheetah cubs have just started to follow their mother as she hunts and to share her food. The mother is watching for lions, leopards, and hyenas, which could attack her cubs.

After a few weeks the cubs will become very active.

They play near the den, wrestling each other and pouncing on anything that moves. It might be a leaf, a butterfly, or their mother's tail. This play is very important. The cubs are developing the skills and coordination they will need later to catch prey.

By about two months in age the cubs begin eating meat their mother brings, and later they start joining her on trips away from the den. They share her kills and try chasing small animals of their own. Cheetah cubs start joining their mother when they are very young, at about six weeks in age. That is because a cheetah mother must travel long distances to find enough prey. She cannot be tied to a den for long.

A big-cat mother must be good at hunting.

She needs to feed both herself and her growing cubs. At first it can be tricky for the cubs to keep up with their mother. They certainly do not want to lose her. Leopards have a white flash of fur on their tails, which they hold up like a flag for their cubs to follow. Lion tails have a black tip. Tigers have white spots on the back of their ears that may help the youngsters keep sight of their mother.

Things can be difficult for the mother, too. The cubs will scare away prey if they do not behave. A mother leopard or cheetah will swish her tail to tell her cubs to lie still while she hunts. She will lead the cubs to the kill afterward or drag the prey back to them. Sometimes she will bring a live animal to her cubs and release it for them to practice catching, while she looks on.

When a lion cub is about two months old its mother leads it from the den and introduces it to the pride. There it can be protected by other members of the pride. Lionesses share babysitting and may even suckle each other's cubs.

In time the cubs learn which animals are the best prey and how to catch them. **But it takes lots of practice to become a good hunter.** Most cubs will be one to two years old before they are ready to leave their mother. Clouded leopards may become independent as early as ten months. Lions can take about three years.

A female lion cub will often stay with her pride as she becomes an adult. But the young of other big cats leave their mothers. Young females often establish a hunting ground close to that of their mother, while male cubs travel much farther away. Male lions and tigers have been known to wander one hundred miles from where they were born. A male puma observed in Connecticut was found to have walked from its birthplace in South Dakota, more than fifteen hundred miles away.

A tiger's stripes hide it well among long grasses. Each animal's coat has a pattern that is as unique as a human fingerprint. This cub is less than two years old, so it is not yet independent from its mother.

After they leave their mother, the male cubs must survive in unfamiliar surroundings and cross the territories of older adults that may attack them. Young male cheetahs sometimes find safety by sticking together as a group, usually of brothers.

This is called a coalition.

Male lions do the same thing. Together they can better defend themselves and catch bigger prey. This early adulthood is difficult, but if a male survives it may one day find its own territory. Often a young male will take the territory of an older male that has become weak.

By the time the cubs are old enough to mate, they will be expert predators. They will have polished their skills over hundreds of hunts. They will know how to walk in complete silence and stalk within yards of their target without being seen. Experience will have taught them everything they need to be one of the most powerful and skillful carnivores on land.

These cheetah brothers are part of a coalition. They are patrolling their territory, looking for prey and leaving scent messages to warn away rival male cheetahs.

Photographing big cats can be challenging. They
are wary, intelligent, and masters of camouflage.

Some, like the clouded leopard, are so rare and elusive that one could
spend years searching without seeing one. Others, like the Amur leopard,
have been reduced to just a few individuals in the wild.

For this reason, several of the big cats I photographed were captive
animals. But I still had an exciting time searching for others in the wild. My
favorite moments were on safari in Africa. I loved watching the cheetah
brothers on pages 44–45 as they patrolled their territory. They walked
together in perfect rhythm, alert to everything in their environment.

My most memorable experience was photographing the leopard on pages 22–23. We spotted it in a canyon one afternoon and I asked our guides if we could spend the rest of the day quietly observing it. The leopard moved several times as it explored its immediate surroundings, and I hoped it would come into the open so I could photograph it. But it always walked within the cover of tall grasses and acacia trees. Sometimes it vanished from sight altogether and I thought we would lose it, but our guides always seemed to know where it was.

Eventually the sun was close to setting and I realized we were almost out of time for photography. Then, like a miracle, the leopard emerged silently from the undergrowth and sat just yards from our vehicle. It seemed to be enjoying a few minutes of relaxation, basking in the last warmth of the sun before the evening hunt. It was one of those magic moments, and I took my photograph.

Not all cat encounters were so peaceful. One evening we were watching elephants from a boat on the Chobe River in Botswana. Suddenly there was a distressed trumpeting sound in the distance. The whole herd became alarmed and raised their trunks high, trying to catch the scent of danger. Later, as we turned our boat for home, we discovered the reason. A pride of lions had brought down a young elephant that had come to drink. It was a difficult sight, but a reminder of how things are on the African plains. And our sadness was softened by the sight of two tiny lion cubs with their mother. Their lives depended on the pride's successful hunt.

Index

Entries in **bold** indicate photographs.

Further Reading

Hunter, Luke. *Wild Cats of the World: Bloomsbury Natural History*. 2015.

Sunquist, Fiona, and Mel Sunquist. *The Wild Cat Book*. The University of Chicago Press. 2014

    To learn about how Nic created this book, and the books he researched before writing the text, visit nicbishop.com.

Glossary

Carnivore A meat-eating animal that hunts or scavenges other animals for food.

Home Range The area in which an animal lives and moves in search of food, shelter, and a mate.

Predator An animal that hunts other animals for food.

Prey An animal that is hunted by another animal for food.

Territory The part of its home range that an animal may defend from other animals of the same type.